Class Is A State of Mind

A Spoken Word Journey

Beverly Campbell

Brandy Publishing LLC

Contents

Introduction

I didn't write this book because I had all the answers.

I wrote it because I finally understood a question I'd been asking my whole life — what does it really mean to have class?

Growing up, class meant wealth. It meant status. It meant the people who looked down from somewhere higher and made you feel like where you came from wasn't enough. Like who you were wasn't enough.

But the older I got — the more I lived, the more I lost, the more I survived — the more I realized that had nothing to do with class at all.

Real class is a state of mind.

It's not what you own. It's not your title, your neighborhood, or whether people know your name. It's how you carry yourself through the hard things. It's what you choose when choosing costs you something. It's how you treat people who can do nothing for you. It's how you speak to yourself in the AM when the world is asleep and it's just you and everything you've been through.

We all go through trials and tribulations. Every single one of us. But we don't all go through the same ones — and we don't all handle them the same way. That's what makes each person's journey worth honoring.

I've had my share of hurt. My share of disappointment. Things I've never told a single person. Things I will take to my grave — not because I'm ashamed, but because sometimes the most classy thing you can do is carry a pain quietly so it doesn't become someone else's burden. There are wounds that, if spoken, would hurt the very people you love. So you hold them. You suppress them. You rise above them — not for yourself alone, but out of love for others.

And that kind of love — that silent, sacrificial, unrecognized love — changes you.

It puts you in a whole different state of mind.

That is class. Not the kind they sell you. The kind you earn — through every hard thing you survived, every burden you carried alone, every time you chose someone else's peace over your own relief.

This book is for everyone who has been through something they never talk about. The one who shows up strong every day while quietly carrying things the world will never know. The one who was told they weren't enough — and somewhere, on some days, started to believe it.

It's for anyone who ever confused struggle with failure. Anyone who wore a mask so long they forgot their own face. Anyone who came close to giving up and didn't — and never got credit for that decision.

This book is for you.

Not the performed version of you. The real one. The unfinished, still becoming, already enough one.

I hope somewhere in these pages you find yourself. I hope you find the language for things you've felt but never been able to say. And most of all — I hope you walk away understanding what I had to live my way into knowing.

Class was never about where you came from.

It's about how you walk.

1

CLASS IS A STATE OF MIND

A Spoken Word Journey

2

PART ONE

3

The Opening

Class Is a State of Mind

Class ain't what they gave you.

It ain't the name on your door

or the shoes on your feet

or whether your people were *hungry*

when they hit the floor.

It ain't the cut of your cloth

or the zip code where you rise —

class is the filter on your vision,

the tuning fork behind your *eyes*.

Nah —

Class is *internal.*

It's the war you fight in silence

when the world keeps spitting on you

and you choose *purpose* over violence.

It's how you *hear* things —

not just the words cutting through the air

but the *bleeding* underneath them,

the years of damage nobody chose to repair.

It's seeing somebody *shattered*

and not walking past their pieces.

It's carrying your own storm

and still being somebody's *shelter.*

It's knowing your own wounds

and refusing to let the damage *increase.*

Class is raw.

It's *ugly* before it's beautiful.

It's screaming into pillows

so the world thinks you're *invincible.*

It's 3am and broken.

It's broke and *still* standing.

It's every door that slammed in your face

becoming the *floor* you built your landing.

It's biting your tongue

when your tongue wants to *set fire* to the room.

It's choosing to bloom

in the same soil that became your *tomb*.

It's sitting in the lesson

when every bone in your body

is *done*.

When you're tired of being tired

and the finish line ain't even *come*.

It's the pause before the anger.

The grace that lives inside the grief.

It's how you treat the person

who can offer you *nothing* in relief.

See —

anybody can have class on a good day.

Anybody can be graceful

when life is going their *way.*

But show me who you are

when the wolves are at the door.

When the ones who said *I love you*

are the ones who left you on the floor.

Show me who you are

when the rent is late,

when the ones you trusted

slammed every single *gate* —

That's where class lives.

In the *flinch* you swallowed whole.

In the bridge you built for others

through the valley you found *hollow.*

In the fire they tried to bury you in

that ended up *refining your soul.*

Class is a state of mind.

Forged in the places they never see.

It's not rising *above* the pain —

it's rising *because* you refused

to let the pain

define what you could *be.*

So wear it unpolished.

Wear it *scarred.*

Wear it like survival.

Wear it *hard.*

And listen —

I'm talking to the one

who almost didn't make it here today.

The one who rehearsed their smile

before they walked out the doorway.

I'm talking to the one

who gave everything

and got *nothing* back but silence.

Who built people up from rubble

while they were still fighting their own *violence.*

I'm talking to the one

they counted out.

The one they whispered about.

The one who had every reason

to quit —

and *didn't*.

That's not luck.

That's not chance.

That's not just surviving —

That's *class*.

The kind of grace

they don't teach in any school.

The kind of strength

that don't come with any tool.

It comes from *you*.

From the deepest, darkest,

most undefeated part of you

that decided —

Not today.

Not like this.

Not without a fight.

So stand in that.

Own that.

Walk in that light —

Because class

was never about how you arrived.

It's about how you *refused* to let them decide

whether you *survived.*

It's a decision made in the dirt.

Not rising above the pain —

but rising *because* of the hurt.

You're still here.

Still standing.

Still breathing.

Still *becoming.*

And that —

that —

is the most classy thing

you've ever done in your life.

4

The Mirror

Who are you when nobody's watching?

The Mirror

When was the last time

you looked at yourself —

really looked —

not at what they made you

but at what you *are*?

Not the title.

Not the trauma.

Not the version of you

that learned to smile through the *scar*.

The mirror don't lie

even when you need it to.

It shows you everything

you've been running from

and everything

you've been *running to.*

We wear so many faces

before we even leave the house.

The strong one.

The funny one.

The one who holds it down

while quietly falling *apart* —

room by room,

wall by wall,

floor by *floor.*

We perform survival so well

we forget

that underneath the performance

there's still a person

keeping score.

But the mirror —

the real one —

ain't made of glass.

It lives in the quiet.

The AM.

The moment after everybody's gone

and it's just you

and everything you've been

trying to *outrun* at last.

Somebody knows.

You know.

And that knowing —

that raw, uncomfortable,

unfiltered knowing —

is not your weakness.

It is the beginning

of your *growing.*

So stand in front of that mirror.

Let it be *uncomfortable.*

Let it show you the cracks.

Let it show you the places
you buried pieces of yourself
and never went *back*.

The real you —
unpolished,
unperformed,
unafraid —

that's the one worth knowing.
That's the one that's got to lead.

Stand there.
Look hard.
Don't flinch.
That face looking back at you
is everything you'll ever *need*.

The Mask

You learned it young —

how to make your face

say *fine*

when everything inside you

was anything *but*.

They handed you a mask

before you even knew

your own face.

Be strong.

Don't cry.

Don't want too much.

Don't take up too much space.

And you wore it.

God — you wore it *well*.

So well that some mornings you put it on before

you even opened your *eyes*.

But masks are heavy.

Don't let anybody

tell you they're not.

They don't just hide you

from the world.

They hide you

from *yourself*.

So what would happen

if you took it off?

Not for them.

Not for the room.

But for *you*.

You'd remember who you were

before the world

got its hands on *you*.

And that person —

that original,

unedited,

unashamed person —

has been waiting.

Patiently.

Faithfully.

Quietly.

Waiting for you

to come *home.*

✦

Before They Named You

Before they named you

difficult —

you were just honest.

Before they named you

too much —

you were just *full.*

Full of fire.

Full of feeling.

Full of everything

a world that preferred quiet

didn't know how to *hold.*

Before they told you

who to be —

you already *were*.

You were whole

before they convinced you

that you were broken.

You were enough

before they introduced you

to the language of *lacking*.

Their inability to hold you

was never evidence

that you were

too much to *carry*.

It just meant

they weren't *built* for you.

So go back.

Pick up that child.

That wild,

unfiltered,

unafraid version of you

that hadn't learned shame *yet*.

Tell them —

I see you.

I'm sorry it took so long.

We're done shrinking.

We're going home.

And then —

walk forward.

As your whole self.

Your *real* self.

The one that class

was always *built* from.

Who You Were Always Meant to Be

Somewhere between

the first mask

and the last performance —

you lost *yourself*.

Not all at once.

The way you lose daylight —

gradually,

then suddenly,

then you look up

and wonder

where the *light* went.

So you folded yourself

into the shape

of their *comfort*

and called it *survival* —

and it *was*.

Don't let anyone

take that from *you*.

But there was always

something underneath.

Before the first apology

for existing *fully* —

there was *you*.

Wild.

Unfiltered.

Unafraid.

That version of you

never *left*.

They just went *quiet*.

The mirror

was never the *enemy*.

It was the only thing

that kept telling you

the *truth*.

And the truth is this —

You were never too *much*.

You were never too *loud*.

You were just *full* —

full of life

that the wrong rooms

didn't know how to *hold*.

From here —

we show up *whole*.

Cracked and *whole*.

Scarred and *whole*.

Still becoming

and *whole*.

Because the mirror

doesn't need you *perfect* —

it just needs you

present.

That's who you were

always meant

to *be*.

◆

<u>REFLECTION</u>

Identity isn't something the world gives you — it's something you reclaim.

Every mask you wore was a survival tool, not a life sentence.

The work of class begins the moment you stop performing for the room and start showing up for yourself.

That's not selfish. That's the foundation everything else gets built on.

<u>JOURNAL PROMPT</u>

Think about the earliest moment you remember changing yourself to fit someone else's comfort.

Who were you before that moment?

Write a letter to that version of you — what would you tell them?

What would you ask them to hold onto?

5

PART TWO & THREE

6

The Dirt

Where class is actually born.

The Dirt

Nobody talks about the dirt.

They talk about the rising.

They talk about the glory.

They frame the struggle in past tense

like it makes a cleaner *story*.

But nobody sits with you

in it.

Nobody talks about

the Tuesday morning

you couldn't get up.

Not wouldn't —

couldn't.

About smiling at work

with an eviction notice

folded in your *chest.*

About being someone's hero

while you were secretly

begging God

for a reason

to keep *going.*

Nobody talks about *that* dirt.

The kind that gets

under your fingernails

no matter how many times you *wash.*

But here's what the dirt does

that nothing else can —

It shows you

what you're *made* of.

The dirt strips everything

that was never really *yours.*

Every borrowed confidence.

Every performed strength.

And what's left —

what's standing

when everything else

has been *stripped* —

that's you.

The real you.

The part of you

that class

is built *from.*

Don't run from your dirt.

It happened.

It was real.

It was *hard.*

And you survived it.

Not gracefully.

Not perfectly.

Not without breaking

in places

that still feel

the weather *change* —

But you survived it.

And survival —

real survival —

is the most classy thing

this world will ever *witness*.

◆

Rock Bottom Has a Floor

They don't tell you

that rock bottom

has a *floor*.

That there's a moment —

even in the deepest,

darkest part

of the falling —

where something in you

catches.

Not saves.

Not fixes.

Just *catches.*

I've been there.

Not the rock bottom

they make movies about.

The quiet kind.

The kind where nobody knew.

Where you went to work.

Where you answered texts.

Where you showed up to everything

while showing up to nothing —

especially

not *yourself.*

Rock bottom for some people

looks like silence.

Looks like a full calendar

and an empty *chest*.

But the floor —

the floor is where

something *shifts*.

It's the moment

you stop falling

and start *feeling*.

The moment the numbness

cracks just enough

to let one real thing

through.

A song.

A face.

A memory of who you were

before all of this

came for *you*.

And in that crack —

that tiny,

terrifying,

beautiful *crack* —

class begins.

Just a quiet,

unwitnessed,

undefeated —

not today.

◆

What Struggle Taught Me
Struggle taught me things

school never *could.*

It taught me

that people show you who they are

the moment

you stop being *useful.*

That some hands only reach for you

when they need something to *hold onto* —

not to lift you —

to *steady themselves.*

Struggle taught me

that walking away

from what's destroying you

is not giving up —

it's *growing up.*

It taught me

that soft people

are not weak people.

That the ones

who feel everything deeply —

who cry at songs,

who carry strangers' pain,

who love harder

than the world

ever loved them *back* —

those are the strongest

people in any *room*.

Because it takes *courage*

to stay open

in a world

that keeps giving you

reasons to *close*.

Struggle taught me

that you can be grateful

and still be *grieving*.

That healing is not linear.

That some days

you'll think you're over it

and a smell,

a song,

a specific quality of *light*

will take you all the way

back to the *floor* —

and that's not failure.

That's just what it means

to be human and *honest*.

Most of all —

struggle taught me

that class is not something

you perform for the world.

It's something you *practice*

in the private moments.

In how you treat yourself

when you've failed.

In whether you extend to yourself

the same grace

you'd give to anyone else

you *loved*.

◆

What the Dirt Made

Nobody chooses the dirt.

It chooses *you*.

Arrives uninvited.

Unpredictable.

Like a storm

that didn't make

the *forecast.*

Nobody talks about

what that actually *feels* like.

They talk about the lesson.

The blessing in disguise.

But nobody sits with you

in it.

That Tuesday

is where class

gets *forged.*

Not in the victory speech.

Not in the highlight reel —

in the *Tuesday.*

In the getting up.

In the keeping going.

In the choosing —

without applause,

without guarantee —

to try one more *time*.

The dirt strips everything

that was never really *yours*.

And what's left

is the truest thing

you will ever *find*.

What it *made*

is you.

Not the performed you.

Not the comfortable you.

You.

The one the dirt

tried to *bury*

and instead —

planted.

Because that's what dirt does

to things

that were meant

to *grow*.

It doesn't destroy them.

It holds them.

In the dark.

In the pressure.

In the silence

where nobody can see *yet* —

until the season *turns*.

Until what was buried

breaks through the surface

and reaches —

reaches —

toward the light

it always *knew* was *there*.

That's you.

That was always *you*.

Not despite the dirt —

because of it.

✦

<u>REFLECTION</u>

The dirt is not the enemy. It's the classroom.

Every struggle you survived taught you something a comfortable life never could.

Class doesn't come from avoiding the hard seasons.

It comes from walking through them without losing yourself completely.

You didn't just survive the dirt. You graduated from it.

<u>JOURNAL PROMPT</u>

Think about the hardest season of your life — the one that almost broke you.

What did it strip away? What did it leave behind?

And looking back now, what did that season teach you about who you really are?

Write it all down — the ugly parts too. This isn't for anyone else. This is yours.

7

The Silence

What you swallowed to keep going.

The Things I Never Said

There are things

I never said

that lived in me

like *weather.*

Not storms — storms pass.

More like a climate.

A permanent condition.

A low pressure system

sitting in my chest

that I learned to breathe *around.*

I never said

that some days the loneliness

wasn't about being *alone* —

it was about being surrounded

and still feeling like a stranger

at your own *table*.

I never said

how much it hurt

to be the strong one.

How the role was never *offered* —

just assumed.

Just placed on my shoulders

like a coat that didn't fit

but I wore anyway

because taking it off

meant someone else

would *feel the cold*.

I never said I was tired.

Not tired like sleepy —

tired like *worn*.

Tired like a road

that's been traveled so hard

for so long

the cracks have started showing

through the *core*.

But silence has a weight.

And I have been carrying mine

long enough.

These are the things

I never said —

I was scared.

I was lonely.

I needed someone

to ask me how I *really* was

and mean it.

I needed —

I needed.

And that —

saying that —

costs more than you *know*.

But I'm saying it now.

Not because the world

is ready to hold it.

But because I finally am.

✦

Grief Nobody Named

Nobody named it grief

so I didn't know

that's what it *was*.

Grief doesn't always

come dressed in black.

Sometimes it comes

dressed in a Tuesday.

In an ordinary,

unremarkable Tuesday

that breaks you

for no reason

anyone can *see*.

We only make space

for certain kinds of grief.

The kind with caskets.

The kind the world

recognizes as *loss*.

But what about

the grief of a friendship

that dissolved without a *word?*

The grief of a childhood

that wasn't *safe?*

The grief of a dream

you had to bury

just to *survive?*

That grief is real.

It doesn't need

a death certificate

to be *valid.*

You are allowed

to grieve the life

you thought you'd have by now.

The person you thought would stay.

The version of yourself

that got lost

somewhere in the *surviving*.

Because unnamed grief

doesn't disappear.

It just finds other ways

to *speak*.

Name it.

Sit with it.

Let it be exactly as heavy

as it *is*.

Because grief that gets named

gets *smaller*.

Not gone.

Never fully *gone*.

But smaller.

Less likely to run your life

from the *shadows*.

You deserve to mourn *fully*.

So you can live

the same *way*.

◆

What Betrayal Does

Betrayal doesn't arrive like a storm — loud,

announced,

something you can brace *for*.

It arrives like a season *changing*.

Gradual.

Quiet.

Until one morning you wake up

and everything is *different*

and you can't name

the exact moment it *shifted*.

What betrayal does —

and nobody warns you about this —

is make you distrust

your own *judgment.*

Not just them.

You.

And that's the cruelest part.

Not what they did.

But what it does

to the way you see *yourself.*

But here's what

betrayal cannot do —

It cannot take

what you *built.*

It cannot erase who you were

before they got their hands

on your *story.*

Because being open —

being willing to trust,

to love,

to believe in people —

is not weakness.

It is one of the bravest things

a human being can *do*.

You don't carry that.

You grieve it.

You learn from it.

You recalibrate —

but you do not become *hard*.

Let betrayal teach you

discernment —

not *distance*.

Let it sharpen you —

not *close* you.

That's class.

Choosing to stay *open*

after every reason

the world gave you

to *shut down*.

✦

Break the Silence

There is a silence

that has nothing to do

with *quiet.*

It lives in the loudest rooms.

At the fullest *tables.*

In the middle of conversations

where you are speaking and smiling

and perfectly *present* —

and completely *alone.*

You know that silence.

You've been fluent in it

longer than you can *remember.*

But you were never *calm*.

You were *carrying*.

Here is what

nobody tells you

about silence —

It doesn't *protect* you.

It just delays

the *conversation*.

Everything you swallowed

is still *there*.

Not gone.

Not dissolved.

Not handled —

waiting.

So this is the moment.

Not for the room.

For *you*.

This is the moment

you give yourself permission

to say the true thing.

To grieve what never got

a *funeral.*

Because silence

that never breaks

becomes a *prison.*

And you were not

built for a *cage.*

Break it.

Not all at once.

Not for *everyone.*

But somewhere.

For *someone.*

Starting with *yourself.*

Because on the other side

of your silence —

is the version of you

that doesn't have to

carry it *anymore.*

Lighter.

Freer.

More *you*

than you've been

in years.

Break the silence.

You've been quiet

long enough.

<u>REFLECTION</u>

Silence is not the same as peace.

Real peace is not the absence of expression — it's the freedom to express fully without fear. Everything you swallowed to survive had a cost. You don't have to say everything to everyone. But you have to say something to yourself.

That's where healing starts.

<u>JOURNAL PROMPT</u>

What is the thing you've never fully said out loud — not to anyone? The grief you minimized, the hurt you dismissed, the truth you've been carrying alone?

Write it here. All of it. No editing. No filtering. Just the true thing. This page belongs to you.

8

PART FOUR & FIVE

9

The Rise

Not above the pain — because of it.

The Decision

Nobody saw it happen.

There was no audience.

No music swelling

in the background.

No moment that looked

like anything other than

an ordinary *Tuesday.*

But inside —

inside something *shifted.*

Not fixed.

Not healed.

Not suddenly okay —

shifted.

It was the morning

you got up

not because everything was better

but because something in you

decided that staying down

was no longer

an *option.*

Because here's the truth

nobody frames and sells you —

The conditions

will never be *perfect.*

The fear will not disappear

before you *move.*

The validation you've been waiting for

was never coming

from *them* anyway.

The decision is this —

To move *anyway.*

To begin *anyway.*

To rise *anyway* —

not because the path is clear

but because standing still

in the middle of your own life

costs more

than any risk

you could ever *take.*

So you decided.

Quietly.

Without announcement.

Without guarantee.

With shaking hands

and an uncertain heart.

You decided that you

were worth the *effort.*

And that decision —

made alone,

made in the quiet —

changed everything.

◆

Becoming

Becoming is not a moment.

It's a *season.*

Long.

Uncomfortable.

Full of days

where you can't tell

if you're growing

or just *surviving.*

Not who you were.

Not yet who you're *becoming.*

Just — *between.*

And the between

is the hardest place

to *live.*

Becoming means

you will lose people.

Not because you did

anything *wrong* —

but because growth

changes the frequency

you operate *on.*

And some people were only ever

built for the version of you

that was still *shrinking.*

Let them go.

Not with bitterness.

Just — let them go.

You are becoming.

Right now.

In this season.

In this in-between

that feels like *nothing*

but is actually
everything.

Trust the process
of your own *unfolding.*

You are not behind.

You are not broken.

You are not too late.

You are exactly
where the becoming
requires you to be.

◆

For Everyone Who Almost Gave Up

This one is for everyone
who almost *gave up.*

Who came closer
than anyone
will ever *know.*

This one is for you.

The fact that you're still here

is not an accident.

It is not coincidence.

It is not luck.

It is the most powerful

decision you never

got credit *for*.

You stayed.

When staying felt impossible —

you *stayed*.

When the weight was unbearable —

you *stayed*.

You found something

to hold *onto*.

And you *held*.

It means you are

stronger than the strongest thing

that ever came for *you*.

The story is not *over*.

There are mornings

you haven't felt yet.

People you haven't met.

Versions of yourself

you haven't *become*.

You almost gave up.

But you *didn't*.

So rise.

Not because everything is *fixed*.

Rise because you *decided*.

Rise because you *stayed*.

Rise because somewhere

in the deepest part of you

something refused

to let the darkness

have the *last word*.

Let *that* part lead.

From here.

From *now*.

◆

Rise Anyway

Nobody gave you a sign.

No perfect moment

where the fear dissolved

and everything aligned.

You just decided.

Quietly.

Without guarantee.

Without applause.

Your rise looked like a Tuesday.

Like getting dressed

when getting dressed

felt like *climbing*.

Like answering one text.

Like showing up

to your own life

for one more day.

That's rising.

Unglamorous.

Unposted.

Unwitnessed.

And more *powerful*

than anything a highlight reel

could ever *capture*.

Because rising

is not a destination.

It is a *direction*.

Every single day

you choose the direction

again.

I see you.

I know you're tired

in a way

that sleep doesn't *fix*.

But you *did.*

So rise.

Not because the fear is *gone.*

Rise because *you* decided.

Rise anyway.

Imperfectly.

Incompletely.

Without knowing how it ends —

rise anyway.

Because every small,

unglamorous,

unwitnessed step *forward* —

counts.

All of it counts.

◆

<u>REFLECTION</u>

The rise is not a moment — it's a practice.

It doesn't announce itself.

It happens in the small, private, unglamorous decisions you make

when nobody is watching.

Every time you chose to get up, to keep going, to try again — that

was rising.

You've been doing it all along.

You just didn't have a word for it. Now you do.

<u>JOURNAL PROMPT</u>

Think about a time you rose — not the big dramatic kind, but the

quiet kind.

The moment you made a small decision to keep going when every-

thing said stop.

What did that feel like? What did it cost you?

Write about your rise — the real one. The one nobody saw.

10

The Walk

How you carry it forward.

How You Carry It

You've been through it.

All of it.

The dirt.

The silence.

The masks.

The mirrors.

The moments that had no business

leaving you *standing* —

and yet.

Here you are.

The question now

is not what happened.

The question is —

how do you *carry* it?

Not as shame.

Not as a weight

that defines everything that comes *after*.

You carry it as *wisdom*.

As the thing that made you *soft*

in a world that hardens.

Open in a world that closes.

Present in a world

that can't stop looking *away*.

Your experience gave you *eyes*

that most people

spend a lifetime trying to *develop*.

The ability to see past the performance.

To hear what's underneath the words.

To sit with someone in their dirt without flinching —

because you know

what dirt *feels* like.

Carry it with *grace.*

Not the performance of grace —

the real kind.

The kind that costs something.

The kind that says —

I've been broken

and I chose not

to break others

with my broken.

That's the walk.

That's the whole *walk.*

◆

Legacy

Legacy is not

what you *leave* behind.

It's what you *plant*

while you're here.

In the people who watched you

choose grace

when you had every right

to choose *otherwise*.

In the children who learned

what strength looks like

not from your words

but from the way you *moved*.

Legacy lives in the small things.

The way you spoke to people

who couldn't do anything for *you*.

The way you refused

to let what was done to you

become what you *did to others*.

That refusal —

that conscious,

daily,

costly *refusal* —

is legacy.

You don't need a monument.

You don't need a stage.

You just need to live in a way

that makes the people closest to you

better

for having *known* you.

That's it.

That's the whole *thing*.

How you heard people.

How you saw people.

How you survived your own story

without losing your *heart*.

That's the legacy.

That's what *lasts*.

A Letter to the One Still in It

I know you're still in it.

I know some of these pages

felt less like poetry

and more like someone reading

your *private journals.*

So let me speak

directly to you —

The one still in the dirt.

The one still wearing the mask.

The one who read every word and thought —

this is beautiful —

and then thought —

but not for me.

I'm too far gone.

Let me tell you

something true —

There is no too far *gone.*

There is no expiration date

on becoming.

You are not too late.

You are not too damaged.

You are not the worst thing

that ever happened to you.

You are not what they called you.

What they left you for.

What they said you'd never *be.*

You are still *here.*

And as long as you're here

the story can *change.*

Not erase —

change.

The dirt becomes wisdom.

The silence becomes voice.

The rise becomes a walk.

And the walk becomes a *life* —

a real,

full,

unapologetic,

classy life.

I'm rooting for you.

Not the performed version.

You.

The real one.

The unfinished one.

The one still becoming.

That one.

Always that one.

◆

Walk in It

You made it

to the other side

of yourself.

Not the clean side.

Not the finished side.

The *real* side.

The side where you know

what you're made of

because the dirt showed *you*.

You know now.

And knowing

changes the *walk*.

Not the stride.

Not the confidence

performed for rooms

that needed you to seem *unbreakable*.

The walk.

The real one.

The private one.

Carrying everything

you've been through

not as *weight*

but as *wisdom*.

The way you hear people.

The way you see people.

The way you show up —

fully,

honestly,

without the *mask* —

because you finally know

that your real face

was always the most powerful thing

you *owned*.

So walk in it.

Walk in everything you survived.

Everything you learned.

Everything you chose

when choosing cost you *something*.

Walk in it.

Not above it.

Not away from it.

Not pretending it didn't *happen* —

in it.

As your whole self.

Your real self.

Your still becoming

and already *enough* self.

The world needs

what only you

can bring into it.

The one who went through it.

The one who stayed.

The one who rose

when rising had no *audience*.

That is class.

That was always *class*.

And you've had it in you

this whole *time.*

Now go.

Walk.

◆

<u>REFLECTION</u>

This is not the end. It's the beginning of the walk.

Everything in this book — the mirrors, the dirt, the silence, the rise

— was preparation for this moment.

The moment you step forward as your full, unedited, unashamed

self.

Not perfectly. Not without fear. But fully.

That is the walk. That is class.

And you've had it in you this whole time.

<u>JOURNAL PROMPT</u>

What does your walk look like from here?

Not the perfect version — the real one.

What are you carrying forward? What are you leaving behind? And

what does living with class mean to you now — in your own words,

in your own life?

Write your next chapter. It starts today.

11

Conclusion

———

Class Is a State of Mind

26 poems · 5 reflections · 5 journal prompts One journey.

———